Prayers for Lent Easter and Pentecost

Donna E. Schaper

Abingdon Press
Nashville

PRAYERS FOR LENT, EASTER, AND PENTECOST

Library of Congress Cataloging-in-Publication Data

Schaper, Donna.
  Prayers for Lent, Easter, and Pentecost / Donna Schaper.
    p. cm.
  ISBN 0-687-34306-2 (alk. paper)
  1. Lent. 2. Easter. 3. Pentecost. 4. Prayers. 5. Litanies.
  6. Meditations. I. Title.
  BV85.S347 2005
  264'.13—dc22

                                                                        2005013777

05 06 07 08 09 10 11 12 13 14—10 9 8 7 6 5 4 3 2 1

MANUFACTURED IN THE UNITED STATES OF AMERICA

Contents

Introduction

Gleaning as a Spiritual Practice

There is a famous French painting by Millet in which two women stand in a field "gleaning." The poor were allowed in to pick up what the rich didn't take.

Churches on the eastern end of Long Island pick up the potatoes left behind by the picking machines and use them in their soup kitchens. A man who died in New York City left behind a garage full of working toasters, heaters, and blenders; he lived the life of a scavenger. I think of Farm Share in Homestead, Florida, which receives and delivers nationally tons of vegetables "too ugly" to ship. Imagine the pressure on a tomato or a squash: It must look perfect to go to market, just like many of us must look better than we do in order to go to market ourselves.

Gleaning is an environmental practice of some significance. It reduces waste while intensifying pleasure—in yard sales and thrift shops and "white elephant" parties at Christmas. It gives objects second and third lives. Gleaning is an attitude as well as an act. It bends and leans toward resurrection. Trash becomes treasure like cross becomes crown.

Most of us spiritually resemble the too crooked crookneck squash. I think of all the people either on disability or hoping to get disability. Something broke in them. They fell off a roof or a ladder. They had a car accident. They got hurt in a crime. Now

1

they are no longer perfect and can't be sent to market. Gleaners still care about people like this: We go to the field and save them.

Gleaners love Habitat for Humanity's Prison Partnership project. It brings prefab houses to jails and lets prisoners build houses. Gleaners *hate* to see time or people wasted.

We had fifty-five poinsettias left over from the Christmas service. They dried and drooped. I took all of them home, turned them on their bottoms, and now watch my new garden thrive every day. I'm going to add the Easter lilies too. I also took all the pots back to the garden store. They were very happy to have them rather than to see them end up in the you-know-where. These plants had a good life while blooming; they may as well have a good life as dirt.

Most of us hope for the same for our bodies. When they say "ashes to ashes and dust to dust" over us, we hope our bottoms and our ends will turn up good soil. When I think of life after death, I will be able to think of this soil I built, gleaned from the old flowers. Gleaning will keep me in shape for resurrection. Gleaning will keep me in shape for transfiguration: I may really change if I learn to use what others leave behind. Gleaning will keep me in shape for Pentecost, just in case anyone wants to light my fire.

Prayers and Meditations for Lent

(1)

O God, we praise you for the small, simple things:
For music that pierces the chaos of life with joy,
for the health at the edge of sicknesses,
for the moment's quiet in the hours of storm,
for the few that held when the many broke and ran,
for the honest sound in a city of noise.
We praise you for the minor key,
the oblique kindness,
the hidden joy.

God of the moment,

God of the music:

Thank you for those brief, precious times
of peace or joy or sustenance.
Each of these moments we want to last forever,
but they never do.
So we hold each moment tightly in our hearts,
fearing it may never come again,

angry at our fading memories.
We live our lives in constant change
and constant challenge.
And you are there,
in those brief, precious moments,
usually in music—in the brief handshake of note with note,
between and in and through each challenge,
to lift our spirits
and carry us through the rest.

Thank you for letting us make music with each other, for each other, and for you.

Amen.

(2)

For risks not taken,
For fears that paralyze us,
For living shallow when the times are deep,
For forgetting how much you love us, Mighty, Seaworthy God,
Forgive us.
Grant us a rare kind of courage. Teach us to swim and to float.
Let us be eager for the deep water, more afraid of silence than we
are of speech, more afraid of risks refused than risks returned to
the Great Risk-Taker.

(3)

Collect our hopes and deliver them from minutiae for minutes
and moments of relief and gladness. For time wasted poorly, we
confess our sin. For time wasted well, we rejoice. We are so rarely
able to just be; we are so often crazed by a destination. Discipline
us, Holy Sprit, with the calm we see in Jesus. Let us trust the com-

ing of your time, your destination, at your speed. Let us glean the meaning in each passing moment. Wake us in the night with what we forgot and let us be glad to know what it is. Let us be the people on whom nothing is wasted. Amen.

Collect the gifts we bring into one mighty offering capable of transforming measly history into magnificent eternity, worthy of creation and your intention for it. We mark time, make time, "step up" and take time. And all the time you are with us. We speed up, slow down, watch the clock, and forget to turn it forward or back, whichever it is. And all the time all our time is really yours. Focus us, Great Watchmaker, who gave us the gift of time. Let us consciously enjoy it. Amen.

(4)

We are almost always counting. Precious Lord, teach us, soon, to count our blessings. We are in a terrible hurry. We repent over-sleeping and its laziness, insomnia and its anxiety, fogginess and its refusal to focus. We seek vigor and calm and attention. Right us, Holy Spirit. Make us someone Jesus would call friend. Amen.

(5)

No one loves yard sales as much as I do. No one. I am the queen of Saturday mornings. To me the poking and hunting into other people's lives and throwaways is a spiritual experience. I appreciate what they can no longer appreciate. I firmly believe that we all have too much stuff, times three, and that yard sales are a great way to de-clutter. They are also a great way to re-clutter—adding other's discards to our own joyful abundance. Life is a long process of spiritually de-cluttering, letting go, and re-cluttering, taking on. The clutter is a prop for other things—the making of an identity by costume, or a home by accessory. When we spiritually look at what another tosses away, we become more able to toss away ourselves. Simultaneously, there are some things that just can't be let go. We need them. We don't know why. Thrift stores are also a way to God. God really doesn't know how to throw anything away. We of course must learn if we are to avoid becoming permanent slaves of our stuff. But throwing away is not in God's vocabulary. We may enjoy that grace.

(6)

Closets and cellars and attics all hold the parts of us that we don't want on display but also can't get rid of. We may need the size twelve jeans again. We may want to put up that poster of the Dead or the souvenir from the Robbins Island visit. We surely can't throw away what adorned our life in our developmental-stage twenties or thirties. Closets are places where we hide things.

Hiding is always a great risk. Living in the open, without secrets, is always better than playing the game of hide and seek so well that the other children can't find you. When we look at our closet, we need to make sure it has no secrets that God would be willing to reveal with and for us.

Cellars are places where we store our past and the past of our children. Those old report cards will someday have a story to tell. What a privilege it is to have a past and to be able to hold on to it. Unlike immigrants who often have to leave everything they love behind, many of us are quite stable. We pay moving companies to carry our cellars around! What a privilege it is to have a past!

Attics are a place for our future. They contain the hope chests and the old dresses that may yet fit. They are places where children go to play in quiet moments. They are places of great strength and light and openness. Very few attics are completely full. What a wonderful thing to be in a useless room that still has space for new identity and the thoughts of the imagination!

Houses are symbols of us. They are places where we enjoy the art of personal development. Gleaning our identity and giving thanks to God for it is a marvelous way to spend Lent. We might even clean out our attics, basements, and closets. Then again we might learn to enjoy them, just the filled-up way they are.

(7)

Taking out the recycling bins always makes me feel like I am preparing for my death. I too will someday go to the landfill. I too will someday make good compost. So will you. When we say good-bye to the milk cartons and wine bottles, the newspapers and magazines, we are saying good-bye to the week in a physical way. Recycling days are great days to make sure we have said our prayers of thanksgiving—and to get ready for the great Thanksgiving when we will be reused by God.

(8)

Did you ever go to a farm auction? The item for sale is held up by someone while another barks prices at a fast pace. People bid items up or down. Some items are all but given away because no one wants them.

Have you ever been unemployed, for a long or short time? Do you remember what that feels like? Glean the meaning of unemployment—and you will go a long way toward appreciating your job, both in its value and its price.

Certainly not every job is worth keeping. Gleaners know that— and gleaners know that we often don't realize what we have when we have it. We often ignore the blessings of today on behalf of some greed for a better day. Be careful. Life can be a party you miss instead of a party you attend. Learn to glean thanksgiving.

(9)

We never know what we have while we have it. We never glean the glory of our husband or wife or partner. We never glean the full glory of any two-year-old. We spend so much time doing "something else" that our two-year-old becomes a three-year-old becomes a thirty-year-old—and we missed life as it passed by.

Focus us on now, Holy God. Let us learn to love the present moment. Let us be gleaners of the glory of now.

(1 0)

As we move through Lent and as we move through life, some of us get broken. We agree with Paul in Romans 7:19. The good that I would have done I did not and the evil that I would not have done I did.

We find ourselves oddly linked to our own illnesses. If not fully responsible, surely there is reason to search for some culpability. We don't just "get" broken, we break ourselves. We eat wrong, we don't exercise enough, we don't take care of our bodies. Very few of us are immune from worry about our health and what we do and don't do to care for it. We feel the cracks.

Or we find ourselves struck down by guilt as we pass a homeless man holding a sign: "Will work for food." We could have done something before now! We are still full from lunch, a lunch we didn't need, and here he is with nothing. We see Christ in his face and turn our eyes and hope the light turns soon. We may fish in our purse for a few coins but guilt grabs us. We know those few coins won't make that much of a difference. We feel the cracks in our consciences as much as in our bodies.

Whenever we feel our own brokenness and take responsibility for it, we develop spiritual muscles. They have a certain serendipity. We never really know what "garbage" is going to give what gift. What we do know is that life's garbage, the body's cracks, and the spirit's embarrassments do bring gifts.

Let us be the people who see grace in garbage and who carry on. Amen.

(1 1)

Difficulty gives closeness to God that doesn't come many other ways. The poet Rumi asks why, if trouble is such a blessing, we don't charge for it. He understands that cracks in the pottery can be a source of joy just as we know that garbage brings gifts. We learn experientially what Psalm 63 means when it says: Your love, O God, is greater than life. Let us learn to be grateful for difficulty. Amen.

(1 2)

Savior and Friend, you know how much I was hurt by something this week. You know how sad I am. You also know that disappointment and regret grow in me as a fertile field for doubt the size of Thomas's. You also know that the best revenge is not to become like the one who hurt you. Let me rise above hurt and into grace. Let me not become the monster I want to destroy in those who hurt me. And let me find the support I need to live elsewhere. Let me let the church carry me when I can't carry myself. Soon let me become one who carries others as well. Restore me to strength. Increase my faith. Allow me the honesty to know how much I ache. Let me not be afraid of my pain.

(1 3)

Of all the things that need gleaning, that need to be saved from the trash heap of history, surely our overused, overconscious, overobserved selves win the prize. We spend so much time in the trap of self-consciousness. Lead us to self-surrender as the true way of saving ourselves. Let the self fall to the ground. Let it drop lightly. Let it be our servant, not our master. Let us save the good parts and let the others go. Bring us to self-surrender and from there let us re-experience your holy seasons. Amen.

(1 4)

When things do spill in our lives, let us not be surprised. Emptying is as important an action as filling. When a vessel shatters, let it not so much lament as glean new uses. Let it realize its newly expanded openness to embrace the light of the world. Let "broken open" be our theme in this holy season before Easter. Let us not walk away from the crippled, the spilled, or the broken. Instead let us glean the meaning of each and all. Amen.

(1 5)

Depression is merely anger without enthusiasm, a wise person said. If we struggle with depression, let us befriend it instead. If we have lost our enthusiasm, send us on a search for it. Send us to parks where children play and fight over trucks in sand. Send us to junior high lots where kids flirt with each other. Send us to a wedding, even if we haven't been invited. Send us to a rock-and-roll party. Do something with us. Life is too short to be lived without enthusiasm. Let us pick up what most other people throw away—and keep these discards as our joy. Let cheer be our dissent from the way life is. Amen.

(1 6)

For the late shift worker at the nursing home,
The migrant worker whose pay is delayed,
The tired mother who still has to find the shoes before she can put her children to bed,
The father who knows the car is failing but can't bear to tell its truth to a worried family,
The son whose report card is going to be bad,
The daughter whose soccer game is terrible and whose parents can't take the news,
For all people who live in disturbed and deep water, for their fatigue and their persistence through it, we pray.
We ask for courage, for patience, for trust, for the refusal to substitute addictive calms for the real thing.

(1 7)

Help us, O God, to act on what we believe. Help us to act as though the cross is true. Help us to know that we have an underworld of which we are not afraid. We go there to rise. We follow Jesus. We are not afraid of evil because he is not afraid of evil. Lead us not into temptation, and deliver us, surely, from evil.

(1 8)

Help me not blame others for what is wrong in myself. Help me not to blame others for not being sufficiently enthusiastic about me or my house or my garden or my work. Let me instead learn to be excited about others—and therein to keep responsibility close to home. Let me give to others what I want for myself. And in that spirit let me receive the gifts of Jesus. Amen.

(1 9)

When I have to go to other worlds and underworlds of my own, guard my goings in and comings out, O God. Let me remember that I stand in a long line of people who have had to go down to go up. Let my tradition be theirs—and let me be a person who is not afraid of the dark so much as afraid of not knowing the light. "Weeping endures for the night, but joy returns in the morning." Amen.

(2 0)

Hoping for a Sparse Lent

"We think of Bach on the harpsichord; one does not know whether the beauty is in what has been subtracted, or in what has not been added."

—Glenn Gould

(2 1)

Yesterday late in the day we got a call that a grandmother had run over a grandfather holding her eight-month-old grandchild. She just didn't see them. She was going out for groceries. The grandfather was standing in the driveway with the child. Both her husband and her grandson are dead. Family is still being notified. This poor woman has to go on living.

We are all balanced on our own slender life thread. We are each less than a century of one combination of DNA, luck, chance, talents, upbringing, and culture. We don't need Jesus to talk about spilled wine or rent cloth to know that things break. We don't need Lent to tell us that our containers are fragile. We know about spill. We know about tear. We know about things that break at the wrong moment.

(2 2)

Fragility, finally, is not just about terrible tragedy or hyperactive worrywart-ism. Think of a bird's nest. How God could trust baby birds to a pile of little sticks, poised high in trees, I'll never know. But our strong and wonderful houses are not that far away from birds' nests. They look bigger and stronger, but we know they are not. They house us as well as they can. In fact one *New Yorker* cartoon suggests a man who wants a smaller house: "I want fewer walls to defend."

(2 3)

The Web site www.snoflake.com says, "Stuff falls out of the sky and we have to understand it."

We don't know what we have when we have it! Indeed one sure message of Lent is that we might look at what we have when we have it. Jesus puts it as his being new wine. He says that he is with the disciples *now* and that's why they don't need to fast. Now they should feast.

(2 4)

During Lent, let's be sure to not box Jesus up and tie a bow around him. He will escape all our understandings. Too often, if we are social activists, then Jesus is a social activist. If we are lonely, then Jesus is someone who assuages loneliness. If we are oppressed, Jesus is someone who liberates us. Jesus is also the forgiver of our sins when we're obsessed, or our good luck charm when we need to be caressed. There is massive evidence that Jesus is all these things and more to people. The central point, though, is that God in man, Jesus Christ, is not captive to any one of our viewpoints—Mel Gibson's or mine or yours or anybody's. Let us learn to be careful with our Jesus.

(2 5)

Give us Lenten eyes, O God, so that we can turn the forces of evil coming at us back toward themselves. There, with Jesus, we imagine the triumph that can come out of trouble, the good news in the bad news. There we see what the poet said about the broken vessel. It crashed on the floor, leaving itself wide open for something new. Let something new find us, let us live in the transformed now.

(2 6)

"Oh, Great Spirit, whose voice I hear in the winds. . . . Let me Walk in Beauty and make my eyes ever ready to behold the red and purple sunset."
—"Let Me Walk in Beauty," Chief Yellow Lark, 1887

Lent is the time of spring in many parts of the country. Let nature teach us God. Let nature spring us to God. Let nature lengthen us to our full stature. Amen.

(2 7)

Rachel Carson finished *Silent Spring* while suffering from late-stage breast cancer. She knew she was ill but didn't want anyone else to know. She finished the book.

Hear our prayer, O God, that we can finish what we have started no matter what we face. Hear our prayer for finality and fullness and the capacity to suffer well. Amen.

(2 8)

"Beware of allowing a tactless word, a rebuttal, a rejection to obliterate the whole sky."

—Anais Nin

No matter what happens, O God, allow us to be people who can still see the sky. No matter who hurts us, keep us looking up and alive. No matter what happens, keep us alive to the wholeness of creation and not just our part. If suffering be ours, let it be sky filled. Amen.

(2 9)

Music is sometimes a window to God. It carries us "over" to a place of beauty, spirit, and energy. It lets us squint and glimpse beyond the daily chores. It relieves the "time famine" in which so many of us live; it competes with the culture of haste. We relax. We see. We gain perspective.

In music we achieve horizon. We see long. We find ourselves transported by the horizon and the long view to something like peace.

Holy God, the culture of haste has won the battle with us and we don't know how to slow down. We have forgotten. Remind us. Use music. Let us make a date with music we love and let us be soothed by it. Let Lent be a time when we dare to be different, dare to be slow, dare to be calm. Amen.

(3 0)

On the Matter of Debt

Our kids were all home for the holidays. There were the usual squabbles about who had borrowed money from whom and how some people were deadbeats. At any given moment someone was always in the deadbeat category. I got sick of this squabbling and announced, "Aren't we all deeply indebted to each other?" Yes, indeed we are.

(3 1)

We are all under a kind of rubble, like that ninety-seven-year-old Iranian woman, found after the earthquake, alive. Did we not find our life in her life? Is she not someone with whom we would like to share fruit? Do we also not need to rise above the rubble of our lives? Gleaning the glory of life is a matter of rising from the rubble and getting on with it. Lent is a practice run. Let us practice rising from the rubble!

(3 2)

David Allen, author of *Getting Things Done*, argues that most people have about three or four major projects at any given time.

They have fifty or sixty unfinished projects sitting behind these on the front burner. Allen consults with people about how to get things done. He argues that we face the karma of incompletion. He suggests that we clear our mind of all those things we had hoped to do, but have not done. I still have Christmas recipes sitting around, calling my name. Guess what? They aren't going to get done. Some did get done. That's where Allen would focus us. Is this incompletion not a sign of the wandering that comes from not paying attention to the fair distribution of fruit? Aren't there some projects that need to bump above others?

(3 3)

Another approach to Lent is through the school of appreciative inquiry. Instead of hiring a consultant to find out what's wrong in the business or a therapist to find out what's wrong in the family, or waking up every morning overwhelmed and under the rubble, appreciative inquirers start with the question, "What gave me life yesterday?" They avoid "deficit discourse" and work on "asset discourse." What did I do that avoided the karma of over-creativity and over-tasking? What did I do that simply put one foot in front of the other?

(3 4)

Don't fly any faster than your guardian angels can. During Lent, as gleaners, we go slowly. We take simple steps. Speed itself is a part of our problem. It causes us to neglect. The longest journey begins with the first step. It's not the hundredth blow that fells the tree but the force in each of the ninety-nine that came before.

(3 5)

Our Budget for Commitment

Jesus says, "Whoever does not carry the cross and follow me cannot be my disciple." The conversation between Jesus and his fellow travelers is often about how much they want to pay to be a part of him and his world. It becomes a lesson in budgeting. If you're going to build a tower, don't you plan for the cost? If you're going to wage a war, don't you develop a strategy and a budget? Don't you have an exit strategy?

Lent is cross time. How much are we willing to spend on it?

(3 6)

Proverbs 22:1-9

Thorns and snares get in the way of most people. Have you ever just thrown up your hands at the computer or in traffic or in the grocery store? "I can't take it any more!" I know I have said this despairing statement more than once. Every time I do say it, I know I am lying. Indeed I can and do take it some more. I return to the computer, go back to the store, drive my car down the same highway that has stolen way too much time from me already. Proverbs is right: Thorns and snares get in the way of most people.

My secretary and I, a few jobs back, had a game we played all day long. We would permit five crises. On the sixth, we would flip out and have a joint hissy fit. That way we approved life's snares and thorns and allowed them into our space. Russell Baker, the great American journalist, also said that the average American home has three broken appliances at any given moment.

What keeps us going? Certainly not our triumphs over the trivial. What keeps us going is the sage wisdom that such is life, that thorns and snares are normal. And what keeps us going is that God goes with us, through the trouble, not staying pure or clear or above it, but walking with us. Without God, we probably couldn't take it any more. But because God abides and is with us, we can.

Those who are not wise fight the thorns and snares. We act as if they shouldn't be happening to us. Those who are wise survive them. We understand that roses come with thorns, and we understand that snares can make us strong.

What snares you the most? How can you befriend it?

Holy God, unsnare us and set us free from the little stuff so we can be more yours, more of the time. Amen.

(3 7)

Acts 28:23-31

Some believe and some don't.
Why do some people believe and some don't?

I put a woman into the hospital yesterday. She was, in the legal jargon, "harmful to herself and possibly others." She went willingly. They will let her out in forty-eight hours, and she, already living in the 1930s, will go back to the loneliness and fear that propelled her to the hospital anteroom in the first place. Can a hospital solve fear? Can a hospital touch depression? Especially when the so-called patient says, "I really have nothing to live for now; without my money there would be less than nothing." She is living off the stock market on a retirement income. Her fear has taken her to a place she can't abide any longer. She was already fearful—and the new insecurities had taken her over the top.

Many people take anti-depressants or other mood-enhancing drugs just to stay "up" enough to manage and survive. What might be preferable is for all of us to nurture our capacity to believe. If my friend whose freedom I took away could just have believed a little, she wouldn't have had to crash so hard.

What might constitute a little belief? A refusal to start the walk down the road of depression is one definition. Whenever we hear ourselves saying, "Oh, that's just how it is" or "Those people always/never do that," we can employ our anti-depressants. Always and never are rarely true words. And things are the way they are, but they are surely not the way God wants them to be.

The people who are able to believe rarely believe big. They often believe small, and that keeps them "up" enough to survive the large stuff. This mustard seed approach can even work for those who just can't believe. One step at a time my friend will get out of the hospital and back home. One hard but wonderful step at a time: Such is the road to belief.

What are the obstacles in me to believing the good news? How can I overcome them?

Holy Spirit, come close to us and let us feel the power of your presence. Let us believe what we feel—and grant us enough faith to challenge all our doubts. Amen.

(3 8)

James 2:1-7

Some wear finery; others don't. God doesn't care, but humans do.

One of the hardest lessons of my long life has been to understand how poor people think about clothes. I think about clothes in a strange way. I don't like to buy them because I can never find a store that expresses enough of who I am. Thus, while being perfectly capable of buying just about any clothing I would like to wear, I can never find anything to wear.

I can only shop in thrift shops where there are a great variety of costumes. I can be the many people I am in thrift stores because they don't have an identity.

While in these thrift stores, I see more of poor people than I do on most days.

What do my clothes say about me? How important are they?

Clothe us in the garment of holiness, Blessed God, and let our style be yours. Amen.

(3 9)

Psalm 119:129-136

My heart pants for thy commandments.

Imagine being so hungry for the word of God that we pant. We breathe heavily. We desire greatly. Imagine.

Maybe it's not really so hard to join the psalmist in this longing. Most of us would love a focusing makeover where we knew exactly what we were commanded to do and what God had in mind for us. Instead of being scattered, we would be sure. Instead of hard choices, we would know what to do and do it. Instead of confusion and delay, and moving the papers from one side of our desk to the other, we would act out of a fountainlike center.

The commandments, by the way, have been made pretty clear. We are to love God the most and each other as we love ourselves.

That one rule should cut through all the piles of paper but rarely does.

How can it cut through the confusion today? Pick someone to love and love him or her. Love them in an excellent way. Then tomorrow do the same. Let the rest go by. Just let the rest go. Pretty soon you will stop panting!

What is my favorite commandment?

Great God, you unclutter our lives by giving us commandments and showing us what is important.

Allow us to find our way through the clutter to the commandment, and let us do so today. Amen.

(4 0)

Proverbs 24:13-14

Wisdom is as sweet as honey.

There is a slow food movement rapidly growing in the United States. It started in Italy, where people preserve old recipes and grow a variety of vegetables that are being "generalized" into general food and motors. Tomatoes that taste really good are hard to find. Likewise life!

When we think of God, it might be nice to think of God as a good taste, as this proverb does. God is wisdom, and wisdom is as sweet as honey. God brings good tastes to our mouths.

Indeed, a way to praise God that could be a lot of fun would be to join the slow food movement and be part of a people who want to improve and enhance our taste buds.

How many ways can we know God, preserve God, season God, serve God? How can God's sweetness become our own? Probably by that act of communion where we are literally offered bread and wine as body and blood. Imagine that. A God in whom we participate physically and who physically comes to us as Jesus, the true human.

How odd of God, we might say. How odd of God to be incarnate, *encarnacion* to the Spanish, the coming as meat. But not odd at all if we read this Proverb, where wisdom is as sweet as honey.

Think with praise and thanksgiving of the best meal you have had this year. Think of what it took for you to make it or serve it or enjoy it. Then think of all the people who had a part in it, from farmer to grocer to cleaner upper! Wow. That's wisdom for you, including just about everything in itself. And that's God too, the great includer.

What speeds me up? What slows me down?

Spirit of the Living God, you cause us to be slow because peace and joy are slow. Slow us down and let us taste your splendor. Amen.

(4 1)

Mark 7:31-37

The deaf hear; the dumb speak.

There are many passages about being mute in the gospels. This one is about the deaf mute, one who has been robbed of not just one but two senses. What God does with muteness and deafness is to bring it to sound.

One of Jesus' most wonderful admonitions is the one about letting those who can see, see and those who can hear, hear. We all know we have permission to see and hear and even speak, but Jesus is a radical about these matters. He wants us to use these permissions. He wants us to really use them.

Did you hear the child crying in the grocery store? Did you speak when the mother hit her? Not mean words but kind words to the mother. Could you say, "I've been just that angry myself. Can I help you? Can I give you a break? Do you have a friend?" Could you become less mute and more of an aid to another?

Did you hear the man make the racist remark? Did you open your mouth or were you silent, mute, well protected? Did you hear the meeting start to turn dumb and trivial and just sit there? Or did you help get it back on track?

Are you dumb? Or are you deaf? Or are you the kind of person who knows how free you are—free to speak, free to hear?

What are my handicaps?

Brother Jesus, we all limp and we all miss cues and we all are blind and we all are dumb. And yet, you bless us! Help us to understand how it is you can love our weakness as much as our strength, our incapacity as well as our capacity. Amen.

(4 2)

Let me know the difference between abundance and saturation, the difference between more and less. Let me be someone who is willing to live with the good enough rather than insisting on the best.

(4 3)

A minister giving a sermon at a wedding shocked the congregation, saying that the grass is *always* greener on the other side. There will always be someone prettier, funnier, and smarter—but marriage is not a matter of comparison-shopping. Considering your decision irrevocable allows you to pour your energy into making things better.

Shock me today, O God, into appreciating what I have rather than asking for more. Let satisfaction apply to my relationships and to my life. Amen.

(4 4)

Spiritual De-cluttering

Many of us want to make the simple choices of our lives in more conscious, personally satisfying ways. We want to eat simply and to live simply and to liberate ourselves from clutter. We must say no to some things in order to achieve this simple form of heaven on earth. De-cluttering, for most Americans, means picking ten things that we don't want or can't have or can't do a week on behalf of open time and space for God. In this liberated time, time that is free from guilt for praise, we appreciate God's gifts to us. Can any ten things in our life possibly be as important as this time to appreciate God?

(4 5)

A Meditation on William James's Definition of Conversion

Lest the thought of the sages be wasted instead of gleaned.

"To be converted, to be regenerated, to receive grace, to experience religion, to gain an assurance, are so many phrases which denote the process, gradual or sudden, by which a self hitherto divided, consciously wrong, inferior and unhappy, becomes unified and consciously right, superior and happy, in consequence of its firmer hold upon religious realities."
—William James, *The Varieties of Religious Experience*

(4 6)

A Meditation on William James's Operational Definition of Religion

Lest great thoughts go ungleaned.

"The feelings, acts, and experiences of individual men in their solitude, so far as they apprehend themselves to stand in relation to whatever they may consider the divine."
—William James, *The Varieties of Religious Experience*

Fit my days into this definition.
Let me feel you.
Act for you.
Experience you.

Let me know some solitude.

Let me have a whiff of the divine as it passes me by.

Amen.

(4 7)

Remembering the Mystical Experiences of the Great

"I remember the night, and almost the very spot on the hilltop, where my soul opened out, as it were, into the Infinite, and there was a rushing together of two worlds, the inner and the outer. It was deep calling unto deep. . . . I did not seek Him, but I felt the perfect unison of my spirit with His. The ordinary sense of things around me faded."

—William James, *The Varieties of Religious Experience*

So said William James, who understood how often most of us pass by the mystical as though it were a forgotten potato in the field. He stood still. Bring us to a sense of you, great God. Amen.

(4 8)

A Lenten Meditation on Evil

"Lead us not into temptation, but deliver us from evil."

—Matthew 6:13 KJV

During Lent we try harder than normal to avoid evil. Some of you know about Procrustus, the mythological Greek figure who guarded the gates to Athens. Athens was the center of culture and power and beauty in those days, but to get there you had to pass by Procrustus and his bed. Whatever part of you didn't fit on his one size fits all bed, he chopped off. If you were too tall, your legs went. If you were too short, you stretched. Procrustus is a form of evil called conformity. We are all to be one size and one shape. As we approach this notion of evil, I ask you what part of you was cut off? What did you have to leave behind to fit in this world? What has Athens done to you?

Or let me tell you about Persephone. You know her as the maiden who had nothing to do but pick flowers. She spent life in a meadow just figuring out which ones were most beautiful. All of a sudden one day, on her way to pick a flower way across the field, the earth opens up and she is consumed. She is abducted into the underworld. Many people speak of the lives of adolescent girls this way: they figure out around twelve that they can no longer be either smart or athletic and still fit the bed of marriage and femininity. So they go underground. Many therapists call underground the place where you can't act on what you know, so you stop knowing it. This underground is not just about girls. Many Vietnam veterans went crazy because they couldn't believe what they saw. Their only solution was to go crazy. This abduction of Persephone is any major betrayal that abducts you and takes you to places you never wanted to go. I think of unexpected poverty. Like the man sitting on the beach with his wife, reading the paper, "Maud, we are no longer on vacation; the company folded." Abductions into the underground happen to lots and lots of people. They themselves are not evil. But our responses can be evil. We can let disappointment kill us, or we can find our way through.

Indeed the God of the Underground is Pluto, whose name also means "Great Riches." This is the complaint that is really a request. The anger that is really a begging for relationship. The siege that is really the invitation to salvation. Ah, breakthrough. Evil: when you can't act on what you know, so you stop knowing it. Indeed, I think of mothers who surely know that something has happened to their child when the child is abused by a teacher or a Boy Scout leader or a priest. But why don't they let themselves know what they know? Because they are curving in onto their own power, which is miniscule, and refusing God's power, which would let them not only know what they know but act on what they know. Is it really true that the Roman Catholic

Church did not know what the priests were doing to their children? No, instead, it is knowing something but then denying it because you can't act on it.

Why don't we know evil? Because we can't figure out a way to act our way out of the conformity of not knowing it.

Our souls have been cut off in our own particular Athens. Evil is our cooperation with evil. Good is our knowledge of evil. We are the problem and we are the only solution to the problem.

Before we even bother with the whole armor of God, we have to believe that we need it. Let me tell you about Inanna, a Sumerian goddess. She has precisely the opposite of Paul's experience with the armor. She is asked to take things off. Inanna has a sister who is in trouble in the underworld, and she thinks it will be a cinch to go down and save her. Because she is so much a somebody in the upper world, she thinks the lower world will also obey her will. On the first level on the way down, Inanna is asked to surrender her headdress. At the second gate, she is asked for her necklace. At the third, her breastplate, at the fourth her girdle, and at the last gate she is asked to take off her very gown. Naked and bowed low, she enters the underworld.

This reminds us of nothing so much as going to the hospital. We give up our role, our identity, our jewelry. In county hospitals they put this stuff in a paper bag. We are disabused of any specialness about ourselves at all.

Or is it actually Christ's path to the cross that Inanna is following? He too is stripped of everything only to come out victorious. How does he have the victory? It is not by his earthly roles or upperworld distinctions, but by the power and grace of God.

In Peru, to be a shaman is to expect to be dismembered on your way. Here, many of us think we can get out clean and whole. Ancient myths join the Lord's Prayer to say that isn't so.

Walter Lippman, the great journalist, defines procrustean behavior as a determination to make the evidence fit the theory. Isn't that what we do when we deny evil in our lives? Don't we become procrustean, and chop off part of what we know on behalf of what we hoped would be true?

Instead we might pray with Paul that we become as fearless as we ought to be, that we enter the underworld aware that it brings riches, that we go to the cross aware of resurrection. When we make this decision, this turn, it is like what happens to Persephone at the crossroads. There she meets Hecate, who tells her she can turn toward life or death. She "unrepresses." She opens herself to truth.

At this crossroads, we rise.

(4 9)

So you don't know how to pray . . .

But when a tower falls or a child cries or a sunset amazes . . .
Don't you say, "Oh, My God"?

These prayers are for people who don't know how to pray.

They begin in "Oh, my God."
They begin in fear.
They begin in compassion.
They begin in awe.

Sometimes they stay right there.

Other times fear becomes comfort.
Compassion causes connection, even sparks, even electricity.
Awe is pregnant with awe.

The turn from an exclamation to a prayer is here: We give our fear to God, our compassion to God, our awe to God. We stop just talking to ourselves. We open up the conversation with the Sacred.

Oh, my God, becomes dear God. Instead of shouting into the wind, we direct our selves to the Sacred One. We take a risk that Someone is listening.

We find the pace of grace. We open and unfold to something we thought impossible. We don't just utter lonely exclamation to the world but decide on conversation with it. Sometimes the world even responds—in the form of Spirit or small wind or small voice or satisfaction of our prayer. Prayers are rarely "answered" the way we think they will be; instead, they are most often surprised by an answer to a question we weren't asking. We don't get cured of the cancer so much as freed from it. Our son does not so much come home as we come home to a place deeper than his rejection.

Prayer makes the turn to communication with God—and in that turn, things happen. Fear dissolves. Community builds. Amazement strengthens us. We are surprised at how often we were asking the wrong question in the first place.

Prayers can be prayers of petition.

These are when we ask that fear be released to comfort, for ourselves or for others.

Examples: Lord, teach me to pray.
    God, teach me to listen.
    God, calm me and tame my fears.

Prayers can be prayers of thanksgiving.

God, teach me to know how much I love this child who has scraped her knee.

Hear my thanks for her.
Help me help her, but mostly let her know how precious she is to me, the way I possibly am precious to you.

Prayers can be prayers of desire.

I want to remove myself from the culture of haste and the time famine. I want to be able to catch a sunset or two. I want to be amazed by bird song and frog song. I want to take time for and with God, and if not God, then with nature so that it can bring me hints of God.

I want to be amused more.

Prayer creates in us the pace of grace. We re-rhythm ourselves. We dance to the beat of a different drum. It is the world's heart-beat, God's heartbeat, and the living nature of all creation. We tune our violin to that message. We turn down the sound on the world's messages (go faster, do more, be more, you're no good), and we turn up the sound on God's assurance (you are okay, you're going to be okay, you are held in my arms).

Prayer yields a sustainable life because we get the accent on the right syllable. God is the right syllable. Our cups overflow toward God.

Prayer is the utterance of the heart. It clears the decks so the heart can say something, like "Oh, my God," and mean it. Prayer sweeps our hearts clean. Prayer empties our minds of the small stuff on behalf of the large stuff.

As we learn to pray, we learn to take one breath at a time, one day at a time. When we say, catching our deepest breath coming from our deepest heart, "Oh, My God," we are actually talking to Someone.

(5 0)

A Lenten Discipline of Peace

Do I have a week to pray for peace?

Or am I too busy?

Day One

Stop the heartbeat, hurt beat, fast beat of my heart, and slow me into a posture of hope for the peoples of the world. Remind me that other people have children, that other people have hopes, and that other people have hurts too. Let the hurt dissolve in the great sea of mercy which is you, Holy God.

Today let me carry one other with me in my heart instead of its own trouble. Replace my heart's beat with the world's beat. Amen.

Day Two

Lead me from death to life, from falsehood to truth. Lead me from despair to hope, from fear to trust. Lead me from hate to love, from war to peace. Let peace fill my heart, my world, and my universe. Amen.

—Universal Peace Prayer

Day Three

I am so small, O God, and your world is so large and overwhelming, vast and magnificent. You have created me to be a part of this greatness—remind me what that means today. What is it I can do to really play my part? Even if I don't have a lead, am I not supporting cast for your creation? Let me know. And then give me the strength to do what needs to be done. Amen.

Day Four

I am peace, surrounded by peace, secure in peace. Peace protects me and peace supports me. Peace is in me, Peace is mine—all is well.

Peace to all beings, peace among all beings, peace from all beings. I am steeped in peace, absorbed in peace, in the streets, at our work, having peaceful thoughts. Peaceful words, peaceful acts.
                    —A Buddhist Meditation

Day Five

The world before me is restored in beauty.
The world behind me is restored in beauty.
The world below me is restored in beauty.
The world above me is restored in beauty.
All things around me are restored in beauty.
My voice is restored in beauty.
It is finished in beauty. Amen.
                    —A Native American Prayer

Day Six

Let nothing disturb you.
Let nothing frighten you.

All things pass. God does not change. Patience achieves every-thing. Whoever has God lacks nothing. God alone suffices.
                    —Saint Teresa of Avila

Day Seven

Lord, make me an instrument of your peace. Where there is hatred, let me sow love; where there is injury, pardon; where there is doubt, faith; where there is despair, hope; where there is darkness, light; where there is sadness, joy.

—Saint Francis of Assissi

(5 1)

A Lenten Week of Prayer for Hope

Day One

Everybody says nothing can be done, and too often I believe them.

Turn down their volume in my head and turn up your great promises to high. Let them drown out the rabble and the rubble of despair. Bring me in focus as a hoping human. Amen.

Day Two

Sometimes people hurt me so badly that I don't think I can bother anymore. They say things that aren't true; they gossip; they lie. I don't want to live in their world. Increase in me the patience of forgiveness, the hope beyond the evidence, and the power to love again as though I have never been hurt. You did; Jesus did. Let me do the same. Amen.

Day Three

Help me feel the warmth of your security, O God, when I get scared. Keep me from going cold. When others declare the permanence of the way things are, let me announce alternatives. Let me speak with joy of the way things might be, and keep me from freezing up. Amen.

Day Four

When I get tired, I get detached from my enthusiasm for the time you are bringing, for the great commonwealth promised and secured in Jesus. Let me rest long enough to know that my fatigue is not your fatigue but that of those who would deafen and deaden hope. Keep me able to see who is pulling what string. Amen.

Day Five

Experience is what we get right after we need it. Let me reflect on the realities of my days and our time in such a way that I have a perspective that is more like yours than like "theirs." Let me not side with those who are hoping against hope, but instead let me side with those who are hoping for hope. May the neglected be cared for by my hope and by me. Amen.

Day Six

Depression, O God, is anger without enthusiasm. Keep my anger enthused at those who hurt others, those who believe nothing can be done to improve schools or to keep the lights on in children's eyes, those who insult the power of your creation with their own smallness. Keep me from the hole of depression and keep my anger alive. Amen.

Day Seven

"Hope," Emily Dickinson said, "is the thing with feathers." Let my hope be light enough to fly. Amen.

(5 2)

A Week of Spiritual De-cluttering During Lent

If you ask people why they don't have a deeper relationship with God, most will tell you they don't have time. Let's get rid of that excuse.

I live in two kinds of worlds and two kinds of time. In one, I cherish the minute it takes me to carry the compost to my composter, which is through the garage, through the garden on the other side of two locked doors. I get to walk through my garden. I get to see the birds, see the sky, and feel the air. I live slowly. I live calmly. I am not pushed nor does anyone push me. I remember God in these times as the one who brings me the calm and makes me glad for birds and sky and air. God nurtures me in these little trips.

In the other kind of world, I do not have time to take the compost to the composter. I need to get to the traffic to get to work to get home to get things done to get to my email to get to the traffic to get to work to get home to get things done to get to my email.

In this world, I develop extensive "messy buildup," that memorable phrase of the children's book series The Berenstain Bears. Adults call this buildup clutter: It is the mail we didn't sort yesterday joining the clothes that can't be worn because they have to be cleaned or mended, which both join the list of phone calls, also obligated and not yet made. Not to mention the email and its newly loud siren song.

In this second world, God is part of the guilt. I should be praying. I should be meditating. I should be practicing Tai Chi or doing yoga or doing something to stop staring at the preposterous piles of work on my desk. But I don't have time. Instead, I have duties with which to lash and whip time. God gets squeezed out, and guilt seeps in.

How can we live a more godly life in this kind of world, where clutter is King and we are its subjects? Why do we imagine heaven later instead of heaven now? Heaven is the time and space in which we are close to God. We speak often of how "nothing" can separate us from the love of God, and yet clutter does so separate us. It gets in the way, in terms of both time and space.

The first task is to get a hold of our space—that means the car, the office, the bedroom, and the kitchen. Let the rest of the rooms worship King Clutter. Make some space that is like that clear day on which we can see forever. I "rotary" clean: Every day for at least ten minutes, I de-clutter one of my spaces. No, I don't live in a tidy house! But I do this ritual in order to make sacred space in my space, in order to love and touch and order a space for God and my family to be "at home."

The second task is to get a hold of our time. A day a week for rest and for God is what our tradition calls Sabbath. Maybe it can't be Sunday anymore because we have to work or do the laundry. But even people working two jobs can enjoy mini-Sabbaths, if nothing more than the refusal to work on the bus or the train and taking that time to enjoy God and to pray. People who "never rest" are not only exhausting themselves: They are also sinning. Sabbath is part of the created order. It is "ontological," that big word that means structured into the very base of things. Even God rested. The refusal to rest because "we don't have time" insults God at the heart of God's creation.

Prayers and Meditations for Easter

(5 3)

Jesus is a gleaner—if for no other reason than that he came back to life after death. He wilted. He was tossed onto life's great rubbish heap. But God said no—and brought him back. Those of us who are born again and again understand. What was lost is found. What was blind sees. What was useless finds its use. That is who Jesus is, the one who restores us.

(5 4)

When we put our Easter basket away this year, let us put it away as though this were its last time, as though next year would not be our privilege. Let us glean the grandeur of being able to put sweet things in baskets and being able to eat them. Let us be the kind of people who really enjoy jellybeans and chocolate bunnies. Let our joy in living be ridiculous! Amen.

(5 5)

Send us back to life after Easter as though we were scavengers for salvation. Let us look under every rock and behind every tree. Let us look in the cellar and the attic and the garage. Let us be the kind of people on whom nothing is lost. Let your resurrection be ours—a resurrection of curiosity, of spirit, of interest in life. May we see your salvation everywhere. Amen.

(5 6)

Doubting Thomas! Of course that's the text the Sunday after Easter. How could it be anything else? Fear blocks joy; doubt blocks joy. If anything ever happened to one of my children, I would not be able bear it. If anything ever happened to my best friend, I would no doubt accuse you, Mighty God. Let me appreciate them today the way I would appreciate them if they were gone. Forgive me in advance for all that I fear and doubt instead of thank and tend. Let me touch the wounds—and then take my hand away, and make me live today with doubt and fear and to live here and there well.

In the name of your holy loss that revealed so much gain. Amen.

(5 7)

Bring me down from the mountain of Easter, Blessed One, into the valley of the daily. Holy Spirit, you are a kind of dailiness that makes the ordinary extraordinary. Show us how to live the way you live, one holy step at a time. Let me be one who knows how to measure out glory in teaspoons, manna-like, just enough for a day at a time.

And dedicate this day of mine to the complete coming of your entire realm. Amen.

(5 8)

Use this community of faith as a shelter for all who are lost and alone, furious and fretful, manic and maniacal. Let us be your body in this world, here and now.

Touch the wounds in our sides, O God, as we touch yours in Jesus. And turn all the trouble into triumph, the way your cross became crown one short week ago.

In the name of the Risen Christ whom we doubt and dare and then believe again and again. Amen.

(5 9)

A Litany for Spring in a Church

Leader: Green us, great God, for a spiritual springtime.

People: Give us courage of daffodils so that we poke our heads out of the ground.

Leader: Green us, O God, so that we are young.

People: Give us a spring in our step and a nimbleness of mind.

Leader: Green us, O God, so that renewal becomes our middle name.

All: Let us be born again and again and again. Warm our hearts as you warm the soil. Let us grow and root, flower, and seed—all in your blessed creation greened by the fertile Christ. Amen.

(6 0)

After Easter, we come down again. Down from the crosses we climbed. Down from the heights to which our musically faithful strains raised us, down from the holiday, back into the real world.

Help us see what is real, O God. Let us not confuse reality with drudgery, but instead let us confuse it with a constant and persistent resurrection.

Join us in daily approaches to cross and crown. Let them be simple. Let them be small. Let them be sure, as sure as breakfast and dawn, supper and twilight, trouble and triumph. Connect us to the small resurrections so that we may come to your large one, over and over this year, in many ways. Amen.

(6 1)

When the mystical germ affects us, we move from a sense of "something wrongness" to a sense of "too muchness." We move from a vague sense of wandering in a dark alley, nowhere to go, nothing to do, to a bright road on a bright day with a wiggle in our walk and vigor in our steps. We become more than the wrongness. We see how all that is is right. We get a sense that everything is right with the world.

Does gleaning apply as a verb? Yes. We glean and see what is really going on. We leave behind the eye shadow with which we have blocked out the universe in its reality and totality. We become an Easter people.

(6 2)

Some of us just can't get out of the sense of something wrong. Shame strikes deepest into the hearts of people. While terror and distress hurt, they are wounds, inflicted from outside, which pen-etrate the smooth surface of the ego, but *shame* is *felt as an inner torment, a sickness of the soul.* It does not matter whether the humiliated one has been shamed by derisive laughter or whether he mocks himself. In either event he feels himself naked, defeated, alienated, lacking in dignity or worth.

Each of us knows despondency. We each have times, even after Easter, when the sickness of the soul is ours. Redeem us! Come to us and lift us into the land where, even after shamed, we are brought back to life. Transform us from a people of inner torment to a people of inner joy. Let that joy explode in new life for us. Amen.

(6 3)

Gleaners have good eyes for the meaning of the Resurrection. We focus on the body, not the corpse of Christ. We focus on the liv-ing, not the dead. We even see the living in the dead. We don't know how to throw things away. We see through the throwaway culture to a keeper culture. We keep and guard meanings. We keep and guard those who are neglected. We see the living in the dead. Amen.

(6 4)

It is almost time, late in the season of Easter, so close to Pentecost, for a good reading of John 21. Jesus is not a fly fisher-man. But he does help the disciples catch and lull exactly 153 fish. He roasts some of the fish for breakfast.

Bring us to this kind of Eucharist on a regular basis. Let us learn all there is to know about this metaphor of Jesus as a fisherman, and then let it too go. All human metaphors for the divine are inevitably limp. And how many women can identify with the lonely exploits of fly fishermen? Or commercial fishermen? And who cares? When it comes to getting to know Jesus at Easter, we have to deal with the stories, as they are, where they are dropped, in whatever fields they first grew.

We can complain later. Now just glean. Breakfast. Fish. Eat together. What fun. Amen.

(6 5)

Remind us that the whole armor of Christ is not a bulletproof vest! It is a form of great vulnerability that yields even greater strength. Let me put the whole armor on and be strong in my weakness. Amen.

(6 6)

Four poets point us to Easter musings.

"Each creative act leaves you humble."

—*Gabriella Mistral*

"Work from the dream outwards."

—*Gabriella Mistral*

"I have always run along the edges, like a sandpiper, looking for something."

—*Eudora Welty*

"The most important thing for a writer is freedom from the reader."

—*Flannery O'Connor*

"Bloom in the noise of the whirlwind."

—*Eudora Welty*

"All we can control is what we hold in our arms, while we hold it."

—*Colette*

(6 7)

The Four Easter Appearances

Jesus appears to Thomas and the disciples and with love and gentleness asks them to touch his wounds. Two frightened women declare, "He is not here!" The grave is empty. Thomas was inoculated with faith by touching the wounds. The women were inoculated with faith by their encounter with the so-called gardener at the tomb. Two disciples, Peter and Cleopas, will meet Jesus on the road to Emmaus. They will be "strangely warmed" by this encounter. My favorite of the stories is Jesus appearing in Jerusalem to the fishermen at dawn. He asks them for a broiled fish and eats it. He tells them not to "spiritualize" his resurrection. He is not a Spirit, he says, but a flesh, and in order to prove it he eats a fish. If you count up all the people in these stories, you might get to twenty.

Imagine God trusting the salvation of the world to twenty people. Clearly the strategy is a kind of chemical, not physical, warfare. It is an inoculation. It is a contagion. It counts on Jesus being infected by God, and Jesus infecting others, and those others infecting others. And guess what? It worked. There was no public relations budget. No forcing of the issue by armies or advertising. One believed, then another believed, and then a third. And today we find Christianity a more than vibrant world religion, just now growing with vigor in Africa and Asia and South America that makes the northern continents look small. Positive contagion is the gospel strategy God used to save the world. (By the way, this breakfast appearance is only found in Luke—once again showing how fragile the web is that bore the gospel to earth.)

(6 8)

Many ecologists are teaching us how to think small again. It is a way we have lost. They say that the main reversal in our thinking is to understand just how beautiful small is. In the Resurrection stories, we have God modeling an admiration of the small and the connected. I love the way Jesus faced his doubters, in the flesh, and said, "Touch me. See me." Those of us who would like to fund a massive publicity campaign on behalf of peace and justice might look closely right here. It could backfire.

Another reversal in our thinking is that of prevention. Old ways of thinking have to do with programmatic moppings up of what has gone wrong. I think of the Department of Children and Family Services, or of most medicine. New ways of thinking have to do with creating the bodies and world and children that we want now. One is preventive and long term and focuses on wellness; the other is palliative and short term and focuses on sickness. The very strategy that God uses in the resurrection of Jesus is a preventive, long term, wellness-focused strategy. It inoculates the world with hope.

Good leadership understands this strategy very well. Good leadership makes people's strengths effective and their weaknesses irrelevant. We create teams that balance each other's strengths. If some member of our team or family is detail-crazed and fussy, and another is so large picture that she never met a detail she understood, that is a good team. We just have to render their strengths effective and their weaknesses irrelevant. We can inoculate each other with this kind of thinking as easily as we can inoculate with the old ways. We must be perfect or we have to be gotten off of the team or out of the family. We must be fixed and improved. Yech! Who wants to be fixed or improved? Indeed who can be fixed and improved? Most of us have fairly permanent warts to which we are very attached. In God's world, these warts are accepted.

(6 9)

An Easter Meditation: Bringing Home Treasure

When it comes to the great hope, which grounds our faith, we have dozens of directions we might go. The biblical treasury is full. We can take any passage home and have it renew our entire abode.

A quick view of the Psalms tells us the Resurrection is early foretold as what happens after the Crucifixion: "Weeping may endure for the night but joy comes in the morning." The prophets also foretold it, saying that a Messiah would come and the Messiah would live eternally in the hearts of the people. Christians argue that the Resurrection is accomplished by God's power in creation, Jesus' power as savior, and the Spirit's power over death. It is "proven by" the empty tomb, the angelic testimony, Jesus' enemies, and the appearances. These appearances are the most important—going to Mary Magdalene, the other women, two disciples on the road to Emmaus, Simon Peter, the ten apostles, then again to eleven gathered, to the apostles at the Sea of Tiberias, then in Galilee, to five hundred "brethren," to all the apostles, then to Paul.

The purposes of the Resurrection according to the scriptures are to

Fulfill scripture and set Jesus on David's throne;
Forgive sins;
Justify the sinner;
Give hope;
Make faith real; and
Prove the Messiah's true coming.

What does the Resurrection do?

It takes place now and always, not later.
It gives eternal life, which includes the now.
It delivers from Spiritual Death.
It changes life.
It issues in immortality.
It delivers us from Satan's power.
It is realized in new life.

Are there other resurrections in the Bible?

Yes, there are at least twenty:

The Shunammite's son
An unnamed man in 2 Kings
The widow's son
Jairus's daughter
The widow's only son
Lazarus of Bethany
Many saints
Dorcas

Any one of these biblical treasures can be brought home and read and re-read over and over again. They make us new when the strong faith we found on Easter morning turns into a simple trust in God. There is nothing wrong with simple trust! Sometimes that is all we can manage, all we can scavenge, all we can find in the seeming dustbin of our lives.

We can renew the strength of faith by visiting the scriptures, by becoming the kind of person who is confident that he or she knows them rather than the clichéd, "I don't know much about the Bible" kind.

No one is preventing us from a prismatic view of the Resurrection. We may find our home in any one of these many stories.

Treasure comes through simple scripture. It moves us from simple trust to strong faith. Nothing that anyone has ever said or thought about Resurrection can dare to be wasted: We need it all and more. Otherwise the prism is not complete.

That prism is not just a treasure, but also a treasury. Glean it. Memorize it. Bring the subject up at dinner. Live in the treasury of Easter.

(7 0)

Preaching to the Easter-Only Crowd

A Meditation for Preachers and Others Who Advise Them

There is one big prohibition and a half-dozen permissions when it comes to preaching to the Easter-only crowd. The prohibition is obvious. Make no reference whatsoever to the fact that you haven't seen much of them lately.

That is like yelling at a teenager who has just cleaned up his room by saying, sarcastically, "It's about time."

Reward the positive behavior; do not punish the past. Punishment only works when we catch people in the act: That means we can call them some Sundays at 10 A.M. and get somewhere with negative remarks. When a family or person has come back, it is prodigal time. It is welcome time. It is a time for feast and great joy.

Toe-dippers in Christianity deserve the same respect as the fully immersed. Jesus may even prefer some of these skeptics to those of us who have become self-righteously convinced. As Bishop Spong so rightly says, the "Church Alumni Association" is the fastest growing religious organization in America, even more in numbers than the evangelicals and fundamentalists. If we want to reverse that trend, welcome is advised when strangers shadow and "darken" our doors.

Manners are everything on Easter and other big crowd days. More positively, what we can do is make sure the service is as transparent as possible. It should be simple and short.

The bulletin needs to be readable by someone in the sixth grade. It needs to make sense. There need to be no "little" mistakes, like forgetting the "to stand" asterisk on the last hymn so the newcomer doesn't know to stand, even though the regulars do. There need to be no confusions about standing or sitting whatsoever. There need to be no bulletin bloopers that cause an "irregular" to feel more uncomfortable than he or she already feels.

Think about the irregular as feeling like they are wearing a big sign that says, "I'm new." Think from their side of the pew as the service is prepared. If there is a sharing of the peace or physical time in the service when people greet each other with the kiss or handshake of peace, make sure it is fully explained before it happens.

Also, today is not the time for the preacher to tell everything he or she knows about the Resurrection. Simple is better. Short is best. People who aren't coming to church regularly probably have been bruised by church. Either people or preachers have insulted them. We need to take very few risks in repeating whatever behavior originally offended.

If regular Christians are getting nervous about your manners by now, good. You might want to take a look at a painting as a form of spiritual preparation for the service. I recommend Marc Chagall's painting called "Crucifixion." There we see a jumbo crowd beneath the cross of Jesus. There we find a quiet and meditative way to prepare ourselves spiritually as well as practically for our guests.

Gaze at (Russian Hasidic Jewish) Chagall's crowd and be reminded once again that salvation is "what all flesh shall see together."

Look at that crowd—almost as if the artist knew one day that the six-billionth baby would be born. Look at that crowd with the artist's simultaneity: This is an eternal, not a timed moment.

Or think of Easter and its guests as boarding a jumbo jet. A child speaking three languages will sit ahead of us in claustrophobic community. Gays will sit next to straights on the jumbo jet. The Jesus of love will make room for them all, in a way not even the best preacher can actually imagine. A family of five will occupy the middle seat, all from Cairo, all playing cards and giggling. The boys will be poking each other. Some of the guests will have just discovered that they have cancer. Others will have been beaten by their spouse the night before. Still others will have discovered marijuana in their children's sneakers. We ride this jet, we enter this holy service of the Easter festival all together beneath the cross of Jesus, clutter clutched to our hearts, self-preservation continuing its old drumbeat—in the air, on the ground, wherever. Those who are "in" will try to keep those who are "out" out, but fortunately we will fail because of the size of our salvation.

The cross makes us new. How? In the way we address the person in the seat next to us. The new will come in new relationships, just as Jesus warned eternally, saying that he lived and died so that we might love one another. The new will be in relationships to what we don't know but do want to know about each other. The new will be in little packages, packed tightly beneath the cross of Jesus in urgent expectation.

(7 1)

Meditation for Easter Dawn

It was the first day of the week. This first line in what we now know as the Easter story places it in another time, another culture, and another religion. Sabbath was still Saturday. It had not become the Christian Sabbath yet. The women who went to the tomb were Jews. They were observing Jewish customs. Not only were they being Jewish, in a Jewish calendar, they were experiencing the absolute transition of these days. Sunday would be different once the full magnitude of what was happening was realized. The calendar would shift, as the earth shifted, when the stone rolled away. Understanding this text is helped by setting the scene. "Dawn." "Right before first light." "Early." "An ordinary day." "Two women."

The two-women feature of the story will want special attention after the runaway bestseller *DaVinci Code* and Mary Magdalene showing up on the cover of *Newsweek* and *Time*. How do we show that less was "hidden" about the sacred feminine than we think? We point out that in the key moments of Jesus' life—his birth, his death, and the first communion—a Mary was present. We don't have to go too deeply down the hidden line on Easter! Instead, we can show the mighty trust of God in women as they stand at the empty tomb.

(7 2)

A Meditation for Easter Dawn

The women brought ordinary spices on an ordinary dawn on an ordinary day to anoint and touch an extraordinary body. They knew how "special" Jesus was and is. They were aware. Still their awareness of the extraordinary death of an extraordinary man did not penetrate the commonplace nature of their visit. They arrived at the earliest opportunity. They brought the kind of spices that women—who then served as undertakers and mid-wives—used when they pursued their role of being first at the cradle and last at the grave. Women did these "folk" things in the time before professionalism. They did them together. They didn't pay for these services; they performed these services. While the preacher will want to preach to the women exclusively, there is nothing wrong with taking their presence as a sign from God about the excluded and the neglected. The outsiders handle the big news. God is magnificent for many reasons, including this persistent raising up of the lowly and the low parts of each of us.

All these elements create a kind of calm in the dramatic scene. Ordinary time, ordinary custom, ordinary people—all this calm and commonplace is changed when the women get to the tomb and find the stone rolled away. In ordinary dawns stones don't roll away from tombs. That doesn't happen. In the Jewish religion it doesn't happen.

(7 3)

A Meditation for Easter Dawn

The men in dazzling clothes tell the women that Jesus has risen. The resurrection is presented as though it were always calmly plotted and always assumed. The men act as though the women should not be surprised, even though their calm and commonplace world has just experienced an earthquake. The men then teach the women the prophecies, that he would be handed over, that he would be crucified, and that he would rise. It is possible that the women knew all these prophecies, but unlikely. They couldn't have been that commonplace. Still the women say their memories have been activated and return to the eleven and to all the rest. There is a journey and some movement here that can be evoked in the sermon.

Why only eleven? Why not twelve? Why all the rest? We won't be privileged to know. That the women return to unnamed disciples and that the women are named is an interesting sideline of the story. The women were Mary Magdalene, Joanna, and Mary the mother of James. This combination of specificity and lack of specificity is interesting. Real people join a crowd of people in hearing the first news of Jesus' resurrection. Luke 24:11 sums it up: "These words seemed to be an idle tale, and they did not believe them." We should not be surprised. This tension between belief and experience and disbelief and lack of experience is also central to our contemporary experience of the Resurrection. We are not the women! We are the eleven.

To conclude this version of the story, Peter is sent to confirm. He gets up, goes to the tomb, stoops, looks in, sees the linen cloths by themselves. He returns home, amazed at what had happened. Or was he just amazed at what he had seen?

The story goes from terror to amazement, through the calm and common to the uncommon, involves the crowd in different roles. The women lead the way. The story is best preached as a page-turner, a thriller, a mystery.

Prayers and Meditations for Pentecost

(7 4)

Loving God,

We give you thanks for moments,
for people, for places where we
can pause, connect, mend, and
celebrate, finding your spirit
in our midst.

You have turned the page to a new century. Many good things abound: email, liver transplants, echocardiograms, frozen yogurt—and so much more that we could never mention. Such glory is yours. Even the Hubble, mercifully, is restored and once again peers far into your galaxies. It will be thrown away someday, but more than once it has been restored.

For all that is good and new, we praise you. For all that is ancient and precious, we also praise you. For traditions and ink pens, for the freedom to die at home, for worn shoes that never fail to bring comfort, for both the new and the old and the jazz they make together, we praise you. In youth and age, new guard and

old guard, may all let their guards down and rejoice in their fullness in you.

Let us not consign one minute or stage to the wastebasket but
instead treasure each one.
Amen.

(7 5)

Help us create space for discerning
your call, time to listen to your
still, small voice. Be known to us
in the sharing of our hearts; be
known to us in the promise of what
is yet to be, grounded in the many promises you have already fulfilled.

(7 6)

We are older today than we were yesterday. And some of us are
wiser. And some of us are more cynical. And some of us have
caught the Spirit. And others missed the ball. And all of us had
the same precious day. Anoint our minutes and our hours,
Precious One. Make every one grand and, if not grand, full of
your presence and warmth. Let us "waste" time in the best sense
of the word, in the sense that we treasure its peace and joy.

(7 7)

Draw us fervently, Creator God, to the end of time the way you
want it. Forgive us for not hastening more to your Realm, when
all the children have health insurance and the elderly are not

alone and crying inside. Hasten the time when no life is wasted or ignored. Clarify your purpose in us—and chasten our resistance to your Realm. Hurry, please. Amen.

(7 8)

How do we solve a problem twice our size? Bite off a piece of it every day. Chew it. Enjoy it. Resolve it. Be done with it and move on. That's how. How do we learn to live a gloriously gleaning life? We pick up all the little things and treasure them, piece by piece, step by step, and moment by moment. That's how. Bless us with good process and good development. Let us not get too far ahead of ourselves. Amen.

(7 9)

When something breaks in or around us, we are the people who are not afraid. We know that God can bring gifts to the broken and we stand ready to receive them. Crack us open, Gracious God, crack us wide open. Let us not lament the break so much as be grateful for the new light and air that flows through us. Amen.

(8 0)

Are we meant to carry salvation, feed the children, cure cancer, bear history, open minds, redeem your world? Have you really looked at us lately?

You're not kidding, are you? We, the ones with no rest for the weary, we the ones with no rest for the cheery, we who confuse riches with wealth, knowledge with wisdom, defense for security, *we* are to carry your creation forward with you! You originated our species for partnership with you! We are to cast our nets on the other side and come up with something!

Wow. Forgive us while we stand amazed and renewed and in wonder. And then help us lift those nets to the other side. Amen.

(8 1)

Loving God, we give you thanks for moments, for people, for places where we can pause, connect, mend, and celebrate, finding your spirit in our midst. We give you thanks for today and the way you hold fast to us through thick and thin. Sustain us. Help us keep on keeping on, and show us your way. Amen.

(8 2)

Help us create space for discerning your call, time to listen to your still, small voice. Be known to us in the sharing of our hearts; be known to us in the promise of what is yet to be, grounded in the many promises you have already fulfilled. Teach us patience. Teach us to tolerate your suspense. Teach us resistance to evils, both small and large.

Forgive us for all that we have let go of. Teach us to hang on. Amen.

(8 3)

Anoint our minutes and our hours, Precious One. Make every one grand and if not grand, full of your presence and warmth. Let the little we give here be marked by a generosity of heart and an awareness of beauty. Amen.

(8 4)

Come now to us and turn us toward a new week; give us a hunger for surprise, a refusal of despair, an openness to possibilities that are as sure as your dawn and your sweet-smelling morning jasmine.

Guide us to and through the deep water of living, Great Leader, so that we may be safe in danger, secure in adventures, ready for risks. When we get afraid and want to turn back and forsake you, take us by the hand and touch our fear. Make us more afraid of fear than we are afraid. And grant us your guidance and our ability to follow it.

(8 5)

Connect us to our body and your Body, the church, in this season that warms to Pentecostal fire. We know the knee bone's connected to the—thigh bone; we know that we are one people. Remind me to figure there will be at least one person I don't like at church for what they did or didn't know. Let me approach my pastor in all of his or her imperfection. Let me find out what trouble is teaching me. Let me stay connected over against all the forces that try to pull us apart. When I get to the valley of dry bones, walk me through the trouble to the other side. Amen.

(8 6)

Renew my faith in the unseen order. Assure me that this world's experience is only one portion of the total universe and that there stretches beyond this visible world an unseen world of which we now know nothing positive. Let me see just how small I am and how grand your cosmos is. Let me be riddled by riddles—and not need to be someone who knows or understands it all. Let me be instead someone who is amazed by it "all" and knows the real meaning of the word *wow*.

(8 7)

Blaise Pascal had a vision in which he saw

Fire.

God of Abraham, God of Isaac, God of Jacob,
not of the philosophers and scholars.
Certitude. Certitude. Feeling. Joy. Peace.

Convert us through such a vision, O God. Let us be open to the possibility that you will take us places that we can't even imagine. Let spiritual virtues be ours and spiritual openness be all. Let me be sure not to so much want to "learn" religious faith but to experience it. From time to time, surprise me with your joy and warmth. Amen.

(8 8)

Lead me to a blueprint for my life, one that includes crucifixion, resurrection, transfiguration, and Pentecost. Let me die to my old ways. Let me rise to new ones. Let me suffer without whining. Let me become someone new every couple of days or months—and grant that Spirit to fill me up, wake me up, and shake me up from this day forward. Amen.

(8 9)

Bless the amateur in me, O God. Bless the ways I have a little bit of a lot and not much of anything at all. Bless the pieces. Bless the fragments. Bless the little threads that others might toss but which I treasure. Make a beautiful garment and life of these threads and fragments. Let them patch into meaning, and let the meaning astound those who think that life is dependent on great gifts. Help us all to see that life is dependent on great fragments, gathered together to make a whole. Amen.

(9 0)

Lead us, O God, to the glory in the fragility of our lives. We know how easy it is to break or to break someone. We turn away in our car and terrible things can happen. We forget to pick up our child on time and wound him or her. We want so much to pay attention to everything that matters, while simultaneously to live light and free. Help us. Let us have the Fire of Spirit and the Shiver of Grace. Let us be focused and relaxed simultaneously. Give us peace and excitement, both not either. Distinguish in us good tension and bad tension—as your Son did in living and you did in creation. Amen.

(9 1)

"You have to play the ball where the monkey dropped it," says the Buddhist sage. We may not like where life has placed us. We may not like where our former choices have placed us. We may be surprised at the degree to which chance brought us to where we are and who we are. Grant us a resurrection in the place where we are. Let us learn to play the ball where the monkey dropped it. Let resentment get out of the way and be the only thing we put in the trash.

(9 2)

With the rush of a mighty wind, you came to make a Pentecost people. Rush now to us with a similar invigoration, so that what we give away may also return to us, twice again. Let us give without such certainty and instead with hope. Amen.

(9 3)

If you ask people why they don't have a deeper relationship with God, most will tell you they don't have time. Let's get rid of that excuse. Let's use Pentecost for a change in life and time. Let's notice that there are flames on our head. Let's notice that a mighty wind is always blowing, even when the air is still.

Let's notice what others don't notice. Amen.

(9 4)

Gardens We Don't Own

Any walk through any park in America can yield opportunities for gardening. Litter will surely present itself as will orphan twigs, anarchist leaves, and wily weeds. These may each be ignored or removed, depending on whether we are private property prigs or global citizens. The former argue personal responsibility: "I didn't put it there. I won't pick it up." The latter argue a broad sense of home: "The earth is our mother. We must take care of her."

I stand firmly in the middle. I weary from picking up other people's trash. Simultaneously, I weary from the selfishness of the litterbugs. I want to do something about them. This double fatigue of the eye and the spirit, these multiple offenses to beauty have caused me to develop a socialist, selfish strategy. Every other public park I use I improve. One day I will walk with impunity through all. The next time and turn I will weed, and gather sticks for my insatiable dog or home fire. I will locate a corner where I can remove all litter and make it look as good as any corner of my home gardens.

Compromise has long been my middle name and the name of my middle.

Imagine solutions to family disturbances that enjoyed the same both/and. Every other day, and only every other day, would we pick up our husband's socks. Every other day, we would not. When half the people in the meeting or congregation are more excited about the past and the other half are more excited about the future, give a little to both and then shut up. The problem is not yours, but theirs. Stay out of the middle. You need the middle for walks in public parks.

When it comes to health insurance, boldly insist on individual responsibilities for personal wellness, while fully searching for those who are ill. When prices for health insurance rise by 15 percent, split the difference with them.

Many things may not be our fault but are still our responsibility. We may do a little, not a lot, about the world's giant problems.

Pentecost changed everything. Let it change us specifically, actually, and practically. Amen.

(9 5)

The great playwright Oscar Wilde often quipped that he lived in tremendous fear of not being misunderstood. That's right: He wanted to be misunderstood. He did not want to be understood. He thought if people understood him, they would capture him, and he didn't want to be captured.

Jesus may have chosen fire as his Pentecost approach for exactly the same reason. He surely wanted to align with the great elements, and did so throughout his ministry—the water of baptism, the clay and earth of clay jars, the air of the transfiguration. Here he comes through fire to get our attention.

Do we understand it? Or do we pass by as though potatoes were not there, left behind, in the field?

How can we understand these miracles? We can do so by allowing ourselves to be open to God's great mystery. This mystery resides in the simplest and most common of things.

To observe Pentecost all we need to do is notice elemental things.

Earth, air, fire, and water.

(9 6)

To experience Pentecost, consider a poor family in Zaire and their glass of milk. The children were used to sharing the glass and sharing the meager amounts of milk that they received. When the oldest child was handed the glass, he immediately asked, "How deep should I drink?" In a way his question is ours: How deeply shall we drink of the Messiah? How much relationship with him and with the one he calls Father can we stand? How close do we want to be? How much do we want to share? How much do we want to enjoy the cup? Both the cup of suffering and the cup of hope?

Let us drink deeply, O God, of this time after Resurrection, this time of Spirit spread extravagantly all over the place. Amen.

(9 7)

Robert Stone, the novelist, tells what his image of Hollywood is. A man is starving in a desert, and he has been lost for some time. He is starving. He is thirsty. Suddenly, a beautiful limo pulls up and opens the door for him to go in. In the limo, there is water. It takes him to Hollywood. There he is offered a luscious hamburger. He is so hungry that he almost bites into it immediately. Then he sees it: There is an enormous cockroach on the side of the hamburger. Is he going to eat it or not?

Hollywood is different than Jesus. Hollywood is the place where people use you; Jesus is someone who loves you. Jesus offers you a hamburger, a piece of bread and wine with no strings attached. There is no cockroach here—but then again there are also very few guarantees. Jesus is in fact so different from the normal public relations campaign that we can't really describe him except in the simplest and most fundamental terms. He is out of this world! In this world. With him, anything you say will be used in your favor.

Because of Jesus' great mystery, we have to have Pentecost. We have to have these vague, fuzzy notions like Spirit.

Let Spirit come. Amen.

(9 8)

Gather us in a great room with all the people of the world.

Visit us with the flame of enthusiasm, the deep belly fire of justice, and the focus that comes to people who live in Spirit more than we live in flesh. Come to us and change us. Color us. Enliven us. Let the new wine flow. Amen.

(9 9)

Partner me, O God. You know I need a wife to help me. You know I need a friend to understand me. You know I need a God to hold me when I am scared. You know my doubts are nearly as large as my faith. Already today I have solved problems twice my size. I tried to make it look easy. I failed. Mother me, O God. People who look as strong and powerful as I do need a cradle, too.

We need a place to rest in our doubt so that we may rise in our faith. Father me, O God, and let me feel like a child toward you, one who sees your magnificent, protecting strength. Amen.

(1 0 0)

Gloom we always have with us. It is the residue that doubt leaves in us. Joy requires tending. Tend in us joy—and let us tend it in others. Dispense the gloom easily and puff it away, then breathe in the joy. You promise joy. You even promised joy to Thomas, as he doubted you.

(1 0 1)

"The miraculous is not extraordinary but the common mode of existence. It is our daily bread. Whoever really has considered the lilies of the field or the birds of the air and pondered the improbability of their existence in this warm world within the cold and empty stellar distances will hardly balk at the turning of water into wine—which was, after all, a very small miracle. We forget the greater and still continuing miracle by which water (with soil and sunlight) is turned into grapes."
—from *Sex, Economy, Freedom, and Community* by Wendell Berry

(1 0 2)

Call to Worship (Responsively)

Leader: When there are barriers that seem insurmountable, let this be a place that inspires the human spirit to rise above.

People:	**When those who are underserved feel weakened by their struggles, let this be a place of strength and encouragement.**
Leader:	When those who are injured seek belonging, let this be a place of family and togetherness.
People:	**When those who are injured seek revival, let this be a place of healing and rejuvenation.**
Leader:	When there are troubled times, let this be a place of tranquility.
People:	**When a safe haven is sought, let this be a place of peacefulness and refuge.**
All:	**Let this congregation and this nation remain a place where no dream is ever too large.**

(1 0 3)

What does it mean to be inoculated by faith? It means that we trust the small. We become like gardeners, who know that the smallest of seeds make the grandest of flowers. I think of the great lupine seeds, which are so small you have to scatter them with a mix of sand in your hand. Lupines easily can be a foot tall with an inlay of flowers in several colors that defy the tiling on the great temples in Morocco. We become like a bit of yogurt culture, which can firm up a whole pot of warm milk. Of course, there are negative viruses as well. I think of the way we used to make vinegar, under the sink in a glass jar. The substance used is "mother of vinegar," and I am sure it has a spiritual as well as physical meaning.

Can you remember how that works? A cloud of chemicals is taken from vinegar gone old. It is placed in a combination of water or apple juice or cider or wine, left over from the table after the guests have all gone. As these leftovers become available, we put them in the hidden jar. It all becomes vinegar in contact with the mother.

Congregations and families can be infected that way too. The smallest amount of vinegar, if allowed to contaminate the sweet, can sour the whole barrel. The folk saying is absolutely right: One bad apple can spoil the bunch. Likewise, infection can be positive. One good apple can improve the whole bunch. My point is that God uses small powerful virus-like seeds to get Jesus launched into the world. We become inoculated positively, with faith and hope and love, by Jesus' entry into the world. From there, we become contagious—and spread the news. We try to stop the vinegar—and start the wine.

(1 0 4)

Most people think they know what the first profession was. They are wrong, with all due respect to Mary Magdalene. The first profession was gardening. And gardening knows how to infect the world with hope and beauty. My grandfather grew strawberries and potatoes in upstate New York for a living. He scratched the living out of the ground. He is the reason I like to have dirt under my fingernails and could never really go to a manicurist for fear of derision. From gardening I have learned a lot about positive contagion and negative contagion. Bugs can wipe you out or bugs can help you grow. These tiniest of animals carry a lot of power. Like the little lupine seed, they can go a long way toward beauty and a long way toward devastation. By the way, if anybody knows how to get snails to stop eating the leaves on the lilies, please let me know. I feel like my daily work in ministry is getting the bad bugs to stop eating the good flowers, and so I hate spending evenings picking their slime off my plants.

(1 0 5)

Help me find freedom from too many choices on behalf of happiness. Jesus isn't kidding when he says, "I have come so that you might have abundant life." That means abundant life, not too many choices. There is a time when more becomes less, and most of us are well aware of it. Teach me to hold what I am holding, well, now. Amen.

(1 0 6)

A Meditation on the Valley of the Dry Bones

Ezekiel 37:1-14

We are transported by the Spirit of the Lord to the valley, day in and day out. Ezekiel is not the only one to go there. We are astonished to see that it is filled with a multitude of disconnected and thoroughly desiccated bones. The image is of a battlefield whose slain never received proper burial, but were left to decay (and be ravaged by birds and beasts) where they fell. Having led Ezekiel around these piles of bones, Yahweh asks him a question: "Mortal, can these bones live?" The prophet's response is enigmatic: "O Lord GOD, you know."

Yahweh then orders Ezekiel to prophesy to the bones (as if they had ears to hear!). In response to the prophet's words, the bones are re-membered, bound by sinews, refleshed, covered with skin, and animated by the spirit. The vision proper is followed by an oracle directed to Ezekiel's fellow deportees. The bones, Yahweh informs Ezekiel, are "the whole house of Israel." The exiles are lamenting that their bones are dried up, their hope has perished, and they are utterly cut off. Yahweh instructs the prophet to inform his audience that their present situation and consequent despair will be transformed. God will open their graves, bring them forth from those graves, and return them to their homeland. The Lord will place "my spirit" within the people and they shall live, reestablished on their own soil.

Is this vision one of Old Testament Frankensteinian proportions? Or can we find our life in it? Our dismemberment, our falling apart, our fears, our death? As we head toward Pentecost, let us not be afraid of falling apart. Then let us accept the way you, precious God, put us back together.

(1 0 7)

A Meditation on Unity: Is Unity Good or Bad?

What is this unity like? It is mystical before it is practical. It is what William James describes as the great "muchness" of it all that comes to those who experience God. It is a profound sense that we are connected to God and each other. It is not political so much as it is mystical.

It is also a sense of being linked to larger realities, not just to Greeks or Jews, slaves or frees.

It is, to me, most like morning. It is the inevitability of morning. When we think in mystical union terms, light inevitably follows dark. Dark is not final—nor is light—but they circle around and after each other. We reach for knowledge beyond what we know or experience—and God touches us with that great unity. This is the sense in which unity is good.

Unity can also be difficult! It can be a forced consensus, or a forced harmony, or even a forced homogeneity. Paul in the great Galatians passage is not describing anything that is forced. He is talking about the enormous grace of being able to be yourself while being a part of a group. That is a spiritual and mystical reality.

In my neighborhood, mornings are actually quite hilarious. One of my neighbors, an octogenarian at least, walks his big, black, mean dog with a stick he carries as opposed to a leash. He always says about the dog, "He don't mind." I want to suggest a leash instead of a stick but just bike on by, hoping the dog won't chase me. This gentleman is followed by a man who doesn't really smoke his cigarette. He just keeps it in his mouth and walks by my hedge at such a height and in such a way that only the smoke is visible and the top part of his head. Every morning. Just the cigarette stuck in his mouth. Why do these two people remind me of human unity? Because they are the habit of morning, the great waking up. I see these people as part of the people to which I belong. We all do life in our own way. The third neighborhood character is the man with the parrot. He puts on a business suit, usually by 8:15, puts his parrot on his shoulder and his little dog on a leash, and briskly parades up and down the street.

Unity also implies, mystically, that I am a part of all things. Imagine that!

(1 0 8)

Thoughts for and from the Sick Bed

An old man on his deathbed was very sick. He wanted to die. His crucifixion was his suffering. He had lived too long. As he got closer, he dreamed about gates. They kept opening. He would wake up and wonder if those gates were opened for him. Of course they were.

Maurice Sendak, the great children's author, tells of a time when he was very sick as a child. He spent long hours in his bed. His father tells him that angels will come to visit him when his father can't be at his side. He believes his father but doesn't see the angels.

Then he asks his father why he can't see the angels. I love this because he thinks it is his fault, not his father's, that he can't see the angels. His father has a wonderful answer: If you blink, you miss them. So the poor child spends a lot of time in the bed learning how not to blink. Sure enough, he thinks he masters the art of not blinking—and he sees the angels.

The great Saint Augustine said, "Faith is believing what you don't see—the reward of faith is to see what you believe."

We can't always see unity. Very often, we blink. But with the eyes of the Spirit, not the eyes of the flesh, we become able to see. Even when we are sick, even when we are dying, we are part of the great unity.

(1 0 9)

The Bridge Panic

I was driving back from Boston to Washington. It was a terrible day, rainy and gusty, but I hoped for light at the end of the tunnel. Turnpike! No one knows how much I really hate the New Jersey Turnpike. Thus I took myself off it, on to the Garden State, in hopes of catching a few glances at the ocean, crossing the Delaware Bay on my favorite ferry—and coming in the "back" way to Washington. Most of the time I had was used up in fighting the malfunctioning windshield wipers and the rain. Indeed it was so foggy that I saw nothing but the back of my coffee cup on the crossing of the bay. It got even foggier as I sped toward the Bay Bridge. The Bay Bridge is pretty big. Over fifteen miles long. It was so foggy on this supposed to be wonderful summer day that I didn't even see the bridge coming till I had started up it. By then I was deep in fog, tired from too long a ride, battling failing equipment. (Yes, I know how many of you have had computer struggles over the holiday. Most of us spend most of our days talking to people in India about our computers!) The wipers were actually getting worse. And here I was on the bridge. That's when I realized that three of the four lanes were closed and that I had to stay on the outside lane. Construction!

Does this sound familiar? Too much, too long, failing equipment, foggy, not too much sight. Like that poor Iranian woman who was found alive after five days under rubble? Does this sound like a lot of the life we know? I think so. We tend to get the "lanes closed" challenge right in the middle of the other challenges. We have lives that are often lived under rubble.

But do you remember what that Iranian woman told the stunned doctors after they pulled her out? "I survived because God was with me."

Now I have to tell you that I added to my own problems on the bridge that day because I had a pretty major panic attack while driving on it.

I can't stand heights, even in good weather. I simply gave in to the fear of the experience and let the fear become me. I had no choice but to pray. Many of you have had similar experiences. You got in so deep that you had no choice but to pray. You became so angry that you had no choice but to pray. You got so overextended that you had no choice but to pray. You got so indebted that you had no choice but to pray. You got so buried in rubble that you had no choice but to pray.

My bridge story is a kind of desperate one. I did learn a lot about myself that day. I did realize how fearful I am that we will not be able to bridge all our differences in my congregation. I did realize that I had a deep underground life with regard to bridging and heights and all of that. Most of us do: Most of us could give ourselves to panic in any number of circumstances. We are under rubble. And (not but—and) God is with us. God is there in the beginning and is there now.

Bridge us, mighty God, and stay with us when we are afraid.

(1 1 0)

Joel 2:21-27

Be glad and fear not . . . even addressed to the land and the beasts.

Someone wanted me to be thankful for a grain of sand. I thought that was pretty crazy. She also said I should relax more. Her suggestion for my relaxation was that I lie down in a field and "watch a carrot grow." I thought she was nuts. After all, I have three kids, two cats, a mortgage, and a van. How can I stop to watch a carrot grow inside this lifestyle?

Then I read this passage from Joel. I am to be glad and fear not. And oddly, Joel is addressing not just me, but also the beasts of the field. They are also to be glad and fear not. He even wants the land to be glad and fear not!

In such good company, how could I object? If there is a universal wisdom or a universal way, it is right here. Maximize love and joy; minimize fear. That is a life strategy that works for quick chicken recipes, van-driving moms, those locked up in jail, and those running a revolution. If we maximize gladness in every way, we also minimize fear. Fear doesn't like joy. Fear prefers gloom and doom to joy.

What is fear? It is the assumption that something bad can or could happen.

What is joy? It is the assumption that something good can or could happen.

The beasts and the land rejoice in their lives. We may also.

Haven't you heard a bird sing or seen a blade of grass dance in the wind? Have you not heard the frogs splash into the water and seen the carrots grow? Have you not seen the water slide down the street as if it were at a water slide theme park? That water did not even pay admission or carry a picnic. It just rained on the road in a parade-like fashion.

The beasts and the land rejoice in their lives. We may also.

When was the last time I really relaxed?

Precious Jesus, you who managed time and space without worry, you who imitate the birds and the lilies, draw near, and help us relax in time and space ourselves. Now is all we have. Remind us. Amen.